# Flowers for the Church Year

# Foreword

The church building speaks. Our historical churches are visited and admired by many, and it is important that visitors see evidence of the living church of today as well as the beauty of the building.

Flowers can speak, too. During the services, the mind and heart can be steered quietly towards the message of the day by means of a particular flower arrangement. It may be the colours or the shape of an arrangement which sets people thinking, or sensing a mood, and this can help create the right 'climate' for an atmosphere of worship, praise, sorrow or mystery.

It may be that the flowers and foliage, used in conjunction with a few appropriate objects, start by intriguing people and making them wonder, and end by helping them understand the meaning of the bible passage – such as candle sticks and a menu on a crisp tablecloth to express the parable of a dinner party, for instance, or a child's scruffy lunch box as part of an arrangement expressing the feeding of the five thousand.

If you are new to flower arranging, you may feel the urge to 'play safe' each week and follow a familiar pattern with the flowers and foliage at your disposal. I hope that this book will encourage you to experiment a bit – in fact I hope that eventually you will be dismissing my ideas in favour of far more effective ones of your own!

In the meantime, I have suggested a flower arrangement for you to try each Sunday of the year, apart from Advent and Lent, when traditionally no flowers are used in church. A sketch of the arrangement, and an outline of what it aims to express are also included.

So that you are not working in the dark, it is important for you to know what the theme of each Sunday is. I have provided a short paragraph to explain the main ideas and theme of the day's readings and prayers. If all of you who are involved in this important ministry take time to read this and pray together, the Lord will be able to use what you do for great blessing.

I have aimed to provide plenty of help and encouragement for the beginner, and also freedom for the more experienced to develop the theme in whatever way s/he is inspired.

*Susan Sayers*

# Flowers for the Church Year

A COMPANION TO
ASB YEARS 1 & 2

SUSAN SAYERS

This book is published in 1991 by
KEVIN MAYHEW LTD
Rattlesden
Bury St Edmunds
Suffolk IP30 0SZ

*Flowers for the Church Year*
is extracted from
*Springboard to Worship*

ISBN 0 86209 153 5

Cover design by Graham Johnstone
Typesetting and Page Creation by Anne Hallam
Printed and bound in Great Britain by
Dotesios Limited Trowbridge Wiltshire

# Contents

Foreword   7

BEFORE CHRISTMAS
| | |
|---|---|
| 9th   Sunday before Christmas | 9 |
| 8th   Sunday before Christmas | 10 |
| 7th   Sunday before Christmas | 11 |
| 6th   Sunday before Christmas | 12 |
| 5th   Sunday before Christmas | 13 |
| Advent | 14 |

CHRISTMASTIDE
| | |
|---|---|
| Christmas Day | 15 |
| 1st   Sunday after Christmas | 16 |
| 2nd   Sunday after Christmas | 17 |
| The Epiphany of Our Lord | 18 |
| 1st   Sunday after the Epiphany | 19 |
| 2nd   Sunday after the Epiphany | 20 |
| 3rd   Sunday after the Epiphany | 21 |
| 4th   Sunday after the Epiphany | 22 |
| 5th   Sunday after the Epiphany | 23 |
| 6th   Sunday after the Epiphany | 24 |

BEFORE EASTER
| | |
|---|---|
| 9th   Sunday before Easter | 25 |
| 8th   Sunday before Easter | 26 |
| 7th   Sunday before Easter | 27 |
| Lent and Holy Week | 28 |

EASTER
| | |
|---|---|
| Easter Day | 29 |
| 1st   Sunday after Easter | 30 |
| 2nd   Sunday after Easter | 31 |
| 3rd   Sunday after Easter | 32 |
| 4th   Sunday after Easter | 33 |
| 5th   Sunday after Easter | 34 |
| Ascension Day and Sunday After Ascension | 35 |

## PENTECOST

| | | |
|---|---|---:|
| Pentecost | | 36 |
| Trinity Sunday | | 37 |
| 2nd | Sunday after Pentecost (Trinity 1) | 38 |
| 3rd | Sunday after Pentecost (Trinity 2) | 39 |
| 4th | Sunday after Pentecost (Trinity 3) | 40 |
| 5th | Sunday after Pentecost (Trinity 4) | 41 |
| 6th | Sunday after Pentecost (Trinity 5) | 42 |
| 7th | Sunday after Pentecost (Trinity 6) | 43 |
| 8th | Sunday after Pentecost (Trinity 7) | 44 |
| 9th | Sunday after Pentecost (Trinity 8) | 45 |
| 10th | Sunday after Pentecost (Trinity 9) | 46 |
| 11th | Sunday after Pentecost (Trinity 10) | 47 |
| 12th | Sunday after Pentecost (Trinity 11) | 48 |
| 13th | Sunday after Pentecost (Trinity 12) | 49 |
| 14th | Sunday after Pentecost (Trinity 13) | 50 |
| 15th | Sunday after Pentecost (Trinity 14) | 51 |
| 16th | Sunday after Pentecost (Trinity 15) | 52 |
| 17th | Sunday after Pentecost (Trinity 16) | 53 |
| 18th | Sunday after Pentecost (Trinity 17) | 54 |
| 19th | Sunday after Pentecost (Trinity 18) | 55 |
| 20th | Sunday after Pentecost (Trinity 19) | 56 |
| 21st | Sunday after Pentecost (Trinity 20) | 57 |
| 22nd | Sunday after Pentecost (Trinity 21) | 58 |
| Last | Sunday after Pentecost | 59 |

# Ninth Sunday before Christmas

God created our universe and everything in it, including us. He gives us both physical and spiritual life and sustains his creation with his constant love. As Lord of life he is worthy of all the praise, honour and worship that we can offer.

---

Use bright and varied colours in flower arrangements, and include wheat and dried grasses, fruits and seed pods to reflect the theme of God's glory, and the wonder of the world he has made.

# Eighth Sunday before Christmas

### Today's Theme

The destructive nature of sin separates us from God through our disobedience to his will. It was God's love for us that prompted him to give his only Son so that we could be bought back, or redeemed, from the sentence of death and given the chance of new life in Christ.

---

Use a selection of miniature potted trees if possible, such as orange and lemon (citris mitis), bay, Indian tree of happiness or even a bonsai collection if the parish boasts a bonsai enthusiast.

Miniature gardens in bowls could also be borrowed for today.

# Seventh Sunday before Christmas

## TODAY'S THEME

Real faith is bound to be revealed in action. Abraham was prepared to trust God absolutely, even when he could not understand what he was being asked to do, and God honoured such faith. It is no good talking about having faith in God if we are not prepared to translate it into loving action and obedience to his will.

---

Make one of the flower arrangements an expression of the way God honoured Abraham's act of faith. For Year I, lay down a thick plastic sheet with sand and rocks on it. Pile the sand round the vase so it is hidden. Use yellow and white flowers and dried seed heads in the arrangement.

For Year 2, lay down driftwood or dead branches to be firewood. Place the vase in the centre and lay a length of coiled rope on the wood. Use reds, oranges, yellows and whites to create an impression of fire.

# Sixth Sunday before Christmas

### TODAY'S THEME

God promises to save his people, and he can be trusted to keep his word. Moses had faith in God's promise to set his people free from slavery. Our faith in Jesus can set us free from the binding chains of sin. He will lead us and protect us from evil.

---

Make one of the flower arrangements a foliage arrangement instead, using different types of evergreen. Traditionally, evergreen is a symbol of God's unchanging faithfulness, and today is a lovely opportunity to use this symbol. It is surprising to find how colourful and varied an arrangement like this can be, ranging from the dark, shiny green of laurel, right through to the feathery yellow of the golden cedars.

# Fifth Sunday before Christmas

## TODAY'S THEME

The faithful remnant of God's people, through whom the Good News of God's power and willingness to save is spread to all nations. At every stage of the journey there is bound to be conflict between good and evil, and many will try to lead others astray. But we are to be prepared for this, so that, watchful and alert, we may remain faithful to our calling as followers of Christ.

---

The theme of a faithful remnant will be reflected in a line arrangement, where the eye is led straight up and down a central line of flowers. This is also a practical arrangement for this time of year as fewer blooms are needed. Choose flowers with tall stems, keeping the first one full length and cutting the others progressively shorter. Fill in around the flowers with foliage to give the effect of branching off from the main direction, so that the colour of the blooms looks like a steady, definite path through the distractions. Chrysanthemums would work well, as would Rayonante or Iris.

# Advent

Traditionally there are no flower arrangements during Advent. This makes it a good time to have a good clean out and tidy up. Look at any areas of the church which could be used more effectively; any corners where there is unnecessary junk. Could the library/book shelf be made more attractive and more efficient? Is the children's area working well or could it do with a face lift? We now have four weeks to reshape and reorganise, clean and beautify, both in our lives and our building. A work 'party' lightens the load for everyone, and makes it all more fun. Begin with prayer, have some Christian music on tape to listen to while you work and finish with thanksgiving and light refreshments.

# Christmas Day

## TODAY'S THEME

Christ, our Saviour, is born. Eternal God breaks into human existence to transform and redeem it. In the darkness of night, God's majestic glory becomes a vulnerable newborn baby. Creator of all is entirely dependent on those he has created. Such is the measure of his infinite love.

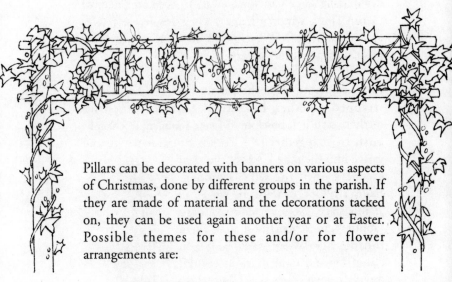

Pillars can be decorated with banners on various aspects of Christmas, done by different groups in the parish. If they are made of material and the decorations tacked on, they can be used again another year or at Easter. Possible themes for these and/or for flower arrangements are:

* Light of the world
* Prince of Peace
* Love came down at Christmas
* Mary, Joseph and Jesus
* Glory to God in the highest

Outside church, a Christmas arch with evergreen and berries is effective. Use a ladder fixed firmly across two poles, and thread greenery throughout.

# First Sunday after Christmas

The great love of God which we can see personally in Jesus, the Christ. All the promises and hopes are fulfilled by the birth of this baby in Bethlehem, because he is the one who can set us free from our slavery to all that is evil. His salvation, beginning in Israel, extends outwards to include every created person.

---

Try making some Christmas swags to decorate pillars or to run along window ledges. They are very effective and make use of the evergreens and berries which are plentiful at this time of year.

I have sometimes seen these made from blocks of 'oasis' strapped together, but this is quite an expensive method, and it is possible to make them more cheaply. First, twist together two lengths of garden wire and weave into them all kinds of pieces of greenery until the wire is hidden. Florist's ribbon can also be woven in at this stage. Now cut cubes of oasis (about 5cm x 5cm) and soak them thoroughly. Wrap each block in clingfilm and tape these at regular intervals down each swag. Into these you can arrange flowers and ribbon, making sure that the oasis is well hidden. Remember too that if the swags are going to be hung on pillars then the flowers will have gravity to contend with! Alternatively, tissue paper flowers can be made and threaded among the greenery. This is also very attractive and has the advantage of lasting longer.

# Second Sunday after Christmas

### TODAY'S THEME

That God's Son, Jesus, shared with us all the experience of childhood. He grew up in a family which had its share of troubles as well as joys, and his love can fill our family life if we invite him to live among us in our homes.

---

Use bright colours and a theme of childhood in the flower arrangements for today. Try incorporating children's toys, such as coloured building bricks or balloons, and picking out the colours in the flowers chosen.

One arrangement could interpret the theme of 'The Holy Family'. One idea for this is to begin with fairly long, 'protective' stems at either side (many evergreens are just right or you could use dried grasses or gladioli). In the centre have small-headed flowers such as dianthus or small pompom chrysanthemums in bright colours. Aim to capture a sense of growth in the arrangement—growth which takes place within the area provided by the outer stems.

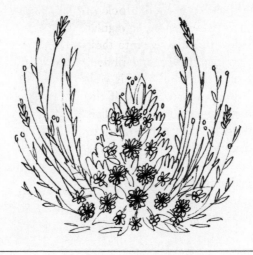

# The Epiphany of our Lord

### TODAY'S THEME

Wise men from distant countries were led to worship
Jesus. The light of the living Christ also leads us, and
when our lives reflect his light, many others will be
drawn to worship the true God who made us and
loves us.

---

Incorporate gold, frankincense and myrrh into one
flower arrangement today. Drape a length of gold
coloured cloth from a pedestal or over a stone step, and
choose flowers to suggest richness and a feeling of
mystery. Flowers with an oriental look are also effective.
Try using eucalyptus and elaeagnus and ivy for foliage,
and chrysanthemums, Christmas roses, lilies or
poinsettia.

# First Sunday after the Epiphany

## TODAY'S THEME

Jesus being anointed at his baptism with the Holy Spirit. When we are baptised we are born again into new and lasting life. We are then given the power and all necessary ingredients for witnessing to God's love wherever he sends us. Together we work towards his kingdom which is founded on caring love.

---

The font can receive special treatment today. Have a predominantly white theme, surrounding the font's rim and foot with cushion arrangements of flowers. You can extend the idea by adding a mirror on the floor, either near the font or at the front of the church. Sprinkle pebbles and shells around its edges and have small arrangements or clumps of potted plants so they look as if they are growing beside a pool. A few tall, overhanging pieces of willow or irises can be very effective, too.

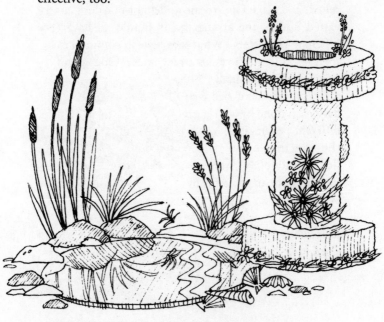

# Second Sunday after the Epiphany

## TODAY'S THEME

The calling of the first disciples. Just as the prophets through the ages and the apostles were called by name by God to work with him for the good of the world, so we are chosen and called to work in partnership with God for the growth of his kingdom.

---

Today's theme of being called by God can be effectively expressed in flowers, so that as soon as people come into church their senses begin to teach and challenge them. Basically, the structure is a circular burst of white, pale yellow and peach coloured flowers to represent God's light. This is mounted on a stool or pedestal. Lengths of white florist's ribbon are fixed under the container so that they radiate outwards and downwards from this 'light'. Each ribbon ends at a small arrangement whose line stretches upwards along the line of the ribbon. These represent those who are called, and since God seems to delight in calling a very varied bunch, the arrangements should all have very different 'characters'. What they have in common is their response to the main arrangement. One way of ensuring that the small arrangements are varied is to have each done by a different person, choosing their own flowers and foliage. Some may have the main stems in evergreens, others in driftwood or dried twigs.

# Third Sunday after the Epiphany

## TODAY'S THEME

God's glory is shown through signs and miracles. Throughout the Old Testament God proves his love for his people by the care and protection he lavishes on them, and as Jesus heals, feeds and encourages his way through the Gospel, we become aware of his glory—the glory of God himself.

---

## Year 1

Capture the wedding atmosphere of Cana with one flower arrangement which includes bridal ribbon, white and pastel shades of flowers, a bottle of wine and a couple of glasses.

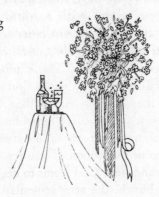

## Year 2

Today's main arrangement develops the theme of the feeding of the five thousand as a sign of God's glory. Include in it bread and silver foil fish, and have the arrangement in a basket, so as to show God's glory being revealed from ordinary things. Include some wheat or dried grasses and try a colour range from brown and orange, through golds and yellows up to creams and whites.

---

# Fourth Sunday after the Epiphany

### TODAY'S THEME

God shows his glory in our lives by renewing us from the inside and transforming us completely. As we increase our availability to the life-giving power of God, we shall become more and more like him, and reflect his glory more and more brightly.

---

In one flower arrangement today have stones or bricks with small pots of ivy, ferns, spider plants etc. tucked in between, along with a number of tiny flower arrangements. The aim is to create a sense of life spilling out of the building materials.

# Fifth Sunday after the Epiphany

### TODAY'S THEME

The wisdom of God, revealed to us clearly in Jesus. Through all the problems and decision-making of our lives we have God's assurance that he will lead us to make good choices and act wisely and well, provided we remain rooted in the loving wisdom of our Lord.

---

Have a very simple, uncluttered line in arrangements this week, to express the purity and integrity of God's wisdom. Suggest the natural world with a few large shells or pebbles, chunks of quartz or other minerals around the base of the flowers. Driftwood and bark are also very attractive and could effectively be incorporated. Try using narcissus, pussy willow or young sticky buds of horse chestnut.

# Sixth Sunday after the Epiphany

### TODAY'S THEME
God's character is revealed through parables to all who
seek to know him more clearly. Jesus often used the
form of parables—stories with hidden meanings—as
an aid to teaching people about God and the Kingdom
of Heaven.

---

Have one arrangement which includes wheat,
interspersed with teasles and thorny twigs. Use
anemones, dianthus, dimorphotheca and cornflowers
among the wheat, so that the effect is of a rich meadow
where all grows together until harvest.

# Ninth Sunday before Easter

## Today's Theme

Christ as the teacher. Not only with his words, but in his life Jesus shows us how to live fulfilled and fruitful lives, realising our potential and playing our part in bringing the world to wholeness.

---

As a central arrangement gather together a selection of spring flowers in pots, baskets of seed and grain and bulbs, branches of forsythia and any other trees and shrubs which are bursting into new life.

# Eighth Sunday before Easter

## TODAY'S THEME

Jesus as the healer. The prophets had foretold the time when God's healing love would renew and restore, and whenever holy men and women became channels of God's power, acts of healing had occurred which directed the people's praise towards the God of creation and renewal. Now, in Jesus, God walks among his people, restoring them to wholeness.

---

'Healing' is the theme of today's flower arrangement. It is a lovely theme to express in flowers and you will probably have lots of ideas of your own! To start you off, here are a few suggestions: a dual arrangement combining the stark, violent colours of pain, contrasted with the green, cream and pastel shades of the peace of healing; flowers of bright and sunny colours arranged in containers such as kidney bowls, with a bandage, small scissors etc; a wheel chair or zimmer walking frame filled with flowers.

# Seventh Sunday before Easter

### TODAY'S THEME

Jesus Christ as the friend of sinners. The bad news about being human is that we seem to find it so easy to hurt one another and indulge in our selfishness; with even the best of intentions, we fail and sin. The good news is that in Jesus, God meets us where we are, loves us, warts and all, and brings about reconciliation, forgiveness and peace.

---

Using deadwood or driftwood, construct a central shape reminiscent of a cross. This will be the basic structure of the flower arrangement, with trailing plants such as ivy, and warmcoloured flowers growing up and around it. You could try using the dark pink dicentra, deep gold narcissus, matthiola or the purple-red malus (crab apple).

---

# Lent and Holy Week

Traditionally there are no flower arrangements during Lent. This gives us another opportunity to clean out and tidy up, perhaps continuing any projects that were started in Advent, such as the library/book shelf or a children's area.

Look also at the outside of the church. Perhaps there are areas here which need clearing and/or reorganising.

Or use the time that would normally be spent flower arranging, in a prayer time or intercession for the parish. Such times of shared quietness are immensely valuable, and in them much spiritual growing goes on. The flowers ministry will be all the richer as a result.

If you are planning an easter flower festival, Lent is a good time to work towards this, and avoid last minute panic.

# Easter Day

Jesus is risen from the dead! Having passed through death to life, Christ has won the victory over everything evil and destructive. Full of glory and power, he enables us to bring the hope and joy of resurrection into the world's problems and tragedies. With God, nothing is impossible.

---

Why not try constructing a festal archway outside the church using two step ladders with a third ladder lashed across the top? Weave plenty of greenery in and out until the main structure is hidden and then decorate with flowers and ribbons Another possibility is to have a festival of flowers in the church this week. Get together a team of about a dozen people to decide on themes and who is going to be responsible for each, ask someone to write labels, and pool ideas and resources. The main theme should be the resurrection; within this, you could either trace God's promises through from creation, the fall, Noah, Abraham, Moses and the prophets; or you could select the main events of Jesus' life. Either way the festival will provide good teaching material both for those involved and for all the visitors.

# First Sunday after Easter

### TODAY'S THEME

The life-giving presence of the risen Lord. The disciples began to realise that Jesus was present with them whether they could see him or not. We, too, experience his spiritual presence among us and welcome him with joy.

---

The whole church continues to look festive this week, with lots of spring flowers; both cut flowers arranged and bulbs in pots. The Easter garden can be kept fresh by sinking small pots and vases into peat below the moss, and replenishing these throughout the Easter season whenever necessary.

# Second Sunday after Easter

### TODAY'S THEME

Jesus leads and teaches us his ways like a good shepherd. We recognise his voice and he knows each of us by name. Just as he led the disciples, on the road to Emmaus, to the point where they recognised him in the breaking of bread, so he leads us, his sheep, to know him and trust him.

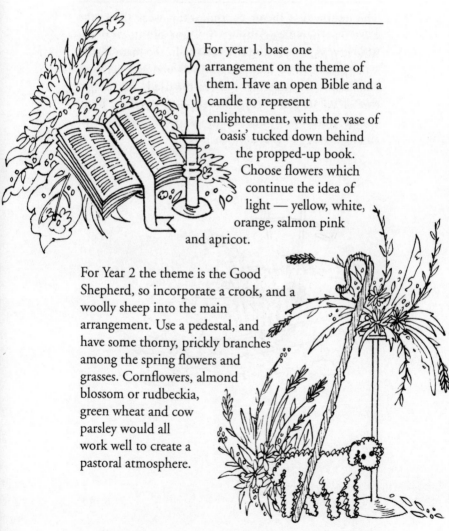

For year 1, base one arrangement on the theme of them. Have an open Bible and a candle to represent enlightenment, with the vase of 'oasis' tucked down behind the propped-up book. Choose flowers which continue the idea of light — yellow, white, orange, salmon pink and apricot.

For Year 2 the theme is the Good Shepherd, so incorporate a crook, and a woolly sheep into the main arrangement. Use a pedestal, and have some thorny, prickly branches among the spring flowers and grasses. Cornflowers, almond blossom or rudbeckia, green wheat and cow parsley would all work well to create a pastoral atmosphere.

# Third Sunday after Easter

### TODAY'S THEME
Jesus is the resurrection and the life. Not only does he live for ever—he is actually life. When we put our trust in him, we become part of that full, complete life, which death will not destroy.

---

The resurrection theme continues this week. Keep the Easter garden flourishing with pot plants and cut flowers replenished where necessary. In the main flower arrangement, hide the base in deadwood and rocks to emphasis new life springing from the dead. Try using a riot of colours of spring flowers—red, yellow, blue, orange, purple and pink—in tulips, daffodils, dianthus, and lilies (such as enchantment).

# Fourth Sunday after Easter

## TODAY'S THEME

Jesus is the Way, the Truth and the Life. As we follow in his footsteps we experience the fellowship of his company, which gives us both courage to do his work and also peace of mind, even when life is difficult.

---

Some churches have a disused door—perhaps a former side entrance—which is never opened. Well, today is a lucky day for unused doors! The famous Holman Hunt picture of Jesus, the light of the world, knocking at the door of our hearts, is based on one of today's readings; it would be very helpful to express the theme in flowers.

Round the sides of the door arrange trailing ivy and wild flowers and grasses, the containers hidden with stones and pebbles. The main arrangement represents the Light of the World. Drape a stand with a length of pale yellow material. Tape a tall piece of 'oasis' firmly in a shallow bowl, so that you can create a circle of flowers, radiating out from a crimson centre. Towards the outer part of the circle, blend the colours through red, orange and gold to yellow. (That may sound offensive, but in fact the effect is a brilliant throb of light—try it and see!)

### TODAY'S THEME

Nothing can ever separate us from God's love. Our new life in the risen Christ is a journey home to the Father, and since God is on our side we need not be anxious and afraid, no matter what may happen to us on the way.

---

Today's arrangements need to express the confidence of walking joyfully 'home' to the Father. Use strong, bold lines and clear, bright colour with flowers such as lilies, dahlia, tithonia and gaillardia.

# Ascension Day and Sunday after Ascension

### TODAY'S THEME

Jesus has ascended into heaven. With his ministry complete, and death conquered, Jesus takes his place at the right hand of God. No longer tied by time and place he reigns in glory.

---

Try decorating the walls and pillars today with bands of flower garlands made like the swags shown in the drawing on page 50. Traditionally the horse chestnut is called the Ascension tree, since its huge clusters of candle-like blossoms are in bloom at this time.

If you have a tree near by, why not use its blossom in arrangements. It would be wise to use wire mesh instead of or as well as oasis, as the branches will be heavy.

# Pentecost

### TODAY'S THEME

The Holy Spirit, poured out on the disciples with a rush of wind and with tongues of fire. Ever since, God's Holy Spirit has enriched and empowered all who open their hearts and minds to receive it.

---

This is always another lovely festival to express in flowers — the theme of the Holy Spirit coming in the form of wind and fire immediately gets the imagination tingling! Colours will be predominantly red, but not exclusively. Introduce orange, peach, gold and yellow as well and create sweeping lines with lots of movement. Ornamental grasses can work most effectively to give the impression of rushing wind.

# Trinity Sunday

### TODAY'S THEME

The God we worship is Father, Son and Holy Spirit. The qualities of God are revealed in the three persons of the Trinity, and in us, too, when we found our lives on him. Filled with his life, the Christian community will be enabled to show the love of God, the grace of Jesus and the fellowship of the Holy Spirit.

---

Try a Japanese-style flower arrangement using three flowers and three twigs or branches. Include some clover or shamrock if it is available. Aim to express the idea of three-ness in one-ness. This kind of arrangement is really a visible meditation, and can be very helpful and stimulating.

# Second Sunday after Pentecost
## (Trinity 1)

### TODAY'S THEME
God's people are called to be united in the fellowship of the Spirit, sharing God's life. But we are given free will, so we can choose whether to be part of God's people or not.

---

For Year 1 the theme of the true vine is a lovely one to express. If possible, use some vines in the arrangement, but if no one grows any, use any trailing plant for the greenery, and include some clusters of grapes as well. Pick out the colour of the grapes with the flowers, and put a pair of secateurs, gardening gloves and a book on growing fruit and vegetables, down at the base of the arrangement.

Year 2 has as its theme the big dinner party to which many are invited but make excuses for not coming. Have a white lace tablecloth draped over the pedestal and some candle sticks and a 'menu' as part of the main arrangement.

# Third Sunday after Pentecost (Trinity 2)

### TODAY'S THEME

Through Christ we die to sin and are raised to full life. Jesus, the Christ, the Son of God, is the fulfilment of the prophecies and the only way to salvation.

---

Make the link between death to the old life and new life in Christ by paying special attention to the font, and the sacrament of Baptism. If your font has a lid, have it raised today, and flowers and foliage spilling out from the font itself. Put garlands round the font's column and surround the base with small flowers, either cut and arranged, or in pots.

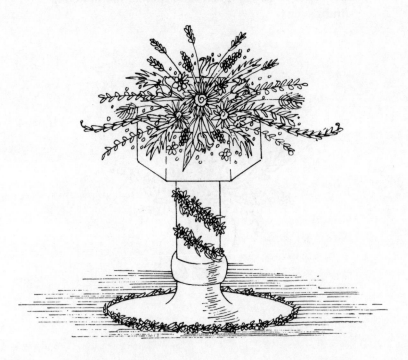

# Fourth Sunday after Pentecost (Trinity 3)

### TODAY'S THEME

The freedom of the children of God which liberates them to serve others. Whenever we deny God through our words or actions it hurts him, because he longs for us to know the freedom and joy of serving him. When we speak and act as his friends there is great joy both for us and in heaven.

---

Try to express the joy of being with Jesus as his friend. An exuberant arrangement with variety of colour and form will create just the right atmosphere. Use an abundance of garden flowers and sprays from flowering shrubs.

# Fifth Sunday after Pentecost
## (Trinity 4)

### TODAY'S THEME

God's Law, summed up in love. It is this law which undergirds us as we work with Christ to draw all people to the creator, by whom and for whom we were made.

---

Some of our ancient churches have the ten commandments painted on the wall. If your church does, accentuate them today, drawing attention to them with a flower arrangement beside or under them. Or have a globe which is enfolded with flowers, to express the love of God which is for everyone.

---

# Sixth Sunday after Pentecost
## (Trinity 5)

### TODAY'S THEME

In Christ we become a new person. As soon as we turn to approach God, he comes to welcome us; he accepts us just as we are and begins to heal our personalities, increase our capacity to love and to forgive, and enable us to become fully ourselves.

---

The restoration and new creation of today's theme is expressed by the story of the prodigal son for Year 1, and by the blind beggar who receives his sight for Year 2. Aim to create an effect of new found hope, incorporating a small arrangement of dried flowers and grasses which leans towards the main display. Choose warm, rich colours and a line which emphasises the welcome.

# Seventh Sunday after Pentecost
## (Trinity 6)

### TODAY'S THEME

Love—the more excellent way of living. God is love, so when we live in love we live in God and he lives in us. In fact, every loving, caring and forgiving act is evidence of God's presence.

---

Today's theme of loving as the best way to live, needs simple, uncluttered arrangements, in which each flower can be seen and enjoyed. Try, for instance, a display of just eight or nine lilies with ivy; or six roses, all of the same colour with twisted willow; or tiny posies attached to the end of each pew in soft mauves and pinks.

# Eighth Sunday after Pentecost (Trinity 7)

### TODAY'S THEME

The fruit of the Spirit. The kind of tree we are will always be shown by the kind of fruit we bear. If we are rooted in Christ, we shall find that our lives blossom and fruit richly.

---

Fruit and vegetables make magnificent displays, and it is a pity to confine them to Harvest Festival. Today's theme of the fruits of the Spirit is a good chance to include some local produce in the arrangements, along with plenty of summer flowers. Try using baskets or trugs as containers, and choose flower colours to enhance the fruit and vegetable colours.

# Ninth Sunday after Pentecost (Trinity 8)

### TODAY'S THEME

Putting on the whole armour of God. On our own we are not powerful enough to fight against evil, but God's power of goodness is sufficient for any evil we may meet, and he promises to give us that power when we put ourselves into his care.

---

To suggest the theme of the armour of God, try using a brass or pewter container today, with rich bronze coloured chrysanthemums and silver or bronze foliage, such as copper beech, bugle or senecio cineraria, eryngium and wormwood.

---

# Tenth Sunday after Pentecost
## (Trinity 9)

### TODAY'S THEME

The mind of Christ. It is, perhaps, his amazing humility which touches us most. For although he understands all things, not only on earth but in the entire universe, and although he is fully in charge, he was prepared to live and die among created beings in order to save them. He, the Lord, serves his people.

---

One way to express today's theme of the mind of God, is to set an arrangement on a mirror. Aim for soft colours and a sense of peace and calm, pure and reflective. Try using a variety of white flowers, with some mauve and blue.

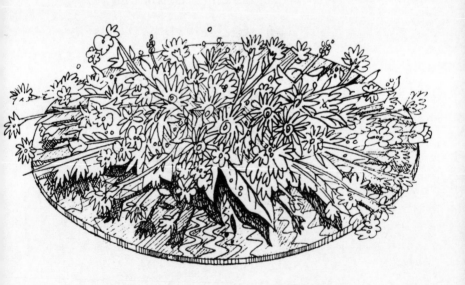

---

# Eleventh Sunday after Pentecost
## (Trinity 10)

### TODAY'S THEME

The serving community. Our belief in Jesus as the Son of God is bound to lead on to serving the world as he did. Through our loving and unflinching service we proclaim to the world the generous, caring nature of God.

---

Today's theme of the way God uses us as channels of his love when we serve others, can be developed by using earthenware containers and sprays of gold and yellow flowers and foliage. Dahlias, yarrow, fennel, roses, and centaurea are all suitable, as are many more at this rich time of year. You could also try a rim of very small gold and yellow flowers along the edge of the altar, arranged in a series of sections of 'oasis'.

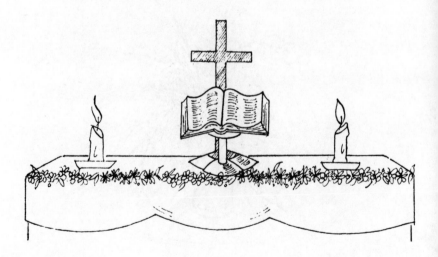

# Twelfth Sunday after Pentecost
## (Trinity 11)

### TODAY'S THEME

The Church as a witnessing community. Since we are the members of Christ's body, it is our witness and example that will either repel or draw others to seek God's face. Unless we display Christ's love, many will never see it.

---

Arrangements today will reflect the theme of witness by being beacons of light and brightness reaching outwards in all directions. Any bright and joyful colours will work well. Try incorporating antirrhinums, delphiniums and gladioli as the expression of light piercing the darkness.

# Thirteenth Sunday after Pentecost (Trinity 12)

### TODAY'S THEME

Just as Christ suffered, so we also will suffer. But the suffering is not negative and demoralising; it is even cause for rejoicing, because through the crucifixion and death of Christ came the resurrection. As we share his suffering we shall also share his glorious life.

---

For today's theme of suffering, try using purples, mauves and crimsons. Sweet peas, roses, sweet scabious, lavatera, delphiniums and stokesia are just some of the flowers around at the moment which would express anguish and sorrow, yet also life and hope. Include some sharp leaved foliage such as holly.

# Fourteenth Sunday after Pentecost (Trinity 13)

### TODAY'S THEME
The family. God loves and cares for us, his children, with parental love, and we are a spiritual family, with Christ our brother. Our own relationships should reflect this strong bond of love and affection; the kind of love which is not possessive but liberating.

---

The theme of the family is a lovely one to express florally. Aim to combine mutual love and support with a sense of fun. You could try this crescent-shaped arrangement which 'cradles' small, bright flowers; or incorporate a child's brick house and pick out the colours of the bricks with the flowers.

# Fifteenth Sunday after Pentecost
## (Trinity 14)

### TODAY'S THEME

Those in authority. All authority stems from God, and when temporal leaders remember this, good government results. Corruption in authority begins when God's supremity is ignored, rejected or usurped. For us, as citizens of heaven through God's grace, loyalty to God's kingdom must always come first; that may well be shown by our loyalty to others in authority.

---

Today's theme of authority springing from God's authority can be expressed in bold, dramatic arrangements with strong lines and colour. Try using chrysanthemums, gladioli, dianthus and the kniphofia variety of red hot poker. Pampas grass, laurel and ferns are useful for foliage.

---

# Sixteenth Sunday after Pentecost (Trinity 15)

### TODAY'S THEME

Loving our neighbour. Since God made all of us—even those we may not like or whose behaviour we may disapprove of—we are to love one another and help those in need, regardless of whether they are friends of ours or not.

To express today's theme of loving our neighbours, try a twin arrangement where two displays interact with one another. Use soft, pastel colours and feathery leaves that produce an open, airy feeling.

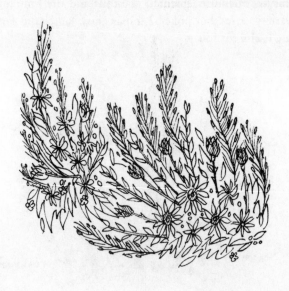

# Seventeenth Sunday after Pentecost
## (Trinity 16)

### TODAY'S THEME

The kind of life we lead proclaims the kind of faith we have. We may say we believe in God, but that is only true if we live a life compatible with belief in the God of love. It will be our kindness, thoughtfulness, self-control and generosity which best prove our faith real.

---

Today's theme of our faith showing in our loving behaviour, would be effectively expressed in this display of three cascading arrangements on different levels. For the main line, choose arching stems, such as tamarisk, willow, forsythia and ivy; sweet peas, asters, cosmos and alstroemeria are among the flowers which look well in this kind of arrangement.

# Eighteenth Sunday after Pentecost (Trinity 17)

### Today's Theme

Offering our lives to God's service. God has given us so much that our thankfulness prompts us to show our love in acts of generosity, both to God in worship, and to one another wherever there is need.

---

To represent the tithe offering of the first fruits, have as the main arrangement either a basket or cornucopia filled with fruits and flowers, spilling out to express both God's bounty and our gratitude. Any seasonal fruits and flowers can be used—the effect is to be a richness and abundance.

---

# Ninteenth Sunday after Pentecost
## (Trinity 18)

### TODAY'S THEME

Living by faith. Faith is what gives us hope and certainty about things we can't actually see. It enables us to step out confidently into the future, and it gives us courage in the face of threats and danger.

---

Year I has the story of Jacob's ladder, as Jacob is led to increased faith; a series of small arrangements at different heights develops the theme. Use white, gold and yellow flowers and aim to create a sense of movement and grace.

Year 2 includes the story of Daniel in the lions' den, so there is lots of scope here! Try reds, orange and gold with powerful lines and spiked shapes to express the fierce lions, contrasted with a foliage arrangement of different green tones to suggest serenity in the face of danger.

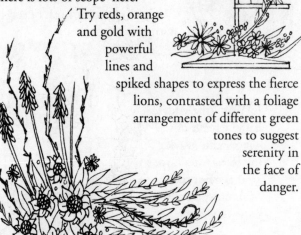

# Twentieth Sunday after Pentecost (Trinity 19)

### Today's Theme

Steadfast endurance. By his own example and encouragement, Jesus inspires us to continue faithful even through the difficult and rough passages of life; in fact, it is often through such perseverance that we are enabled to mature spiritually, and grow to fulfil our potential.

Year 1 uses the burning fiery furnace story to teach about steadfast endurance. Fiery colours for flower arrangements reflect the theme. In the main arrangement, have the 'flames' of flowers and foliage surrounding three yellow lilies. Try incorporating chinese lanterns, burning bush or stags horn.

In Year 2 the athlete's laurel wreath of victory can provide the focus for a flower arrangement today. Aim to express the sense of victory.

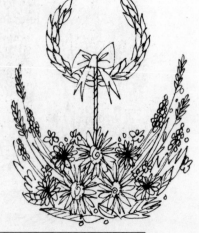

# Twenty-first Sunday after Pentecost
## (Trinity 20)

### TODAY'S THEME

Christian hope. As adopted children of God, we know
that this world and this life is not the whole story. We
are children of eternity, living in the faith that this life
does not finish at death, and our true spiritual home is
in heaven, towards which we are walking as joyful
pilgrims.

---

The theme of today's readings is hope—the joyful
Christian hope of risen life in heaven, so the flowers
need to be full of exuberance and hope. Make the main
arrangement very broadbased, solid and secure, and
'overflowing' as well as uplifting. Choose rich colours
which reflect this idea—chrysanthemums are splendid
and usually plentiful at this time of year. Choose richly
shaped foliage, too, with ferns, rhododendron or richly
coloured autumn leaves.

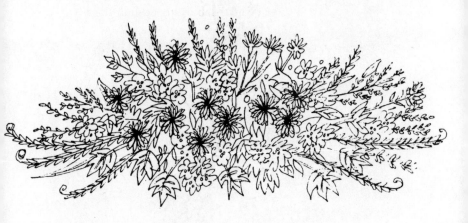

---

# Twenty-second Sunday after Pentecost (Trinity 21)

### TODAY'S THEME

We cannot serve two masters—if we choose to serve God we shall not be able to continue as slaves of money and materialism. We should be as astute about our spiritual lives as the dishonest steward was about keeping his job.

---

The theme of following the narrow path which leads to heaven is expressed in an arrangement with a broad base which tapers upwards into a column. It needs to have an upward sweep in the line, and colours lighten towards the top.

# Last Sunday after Pentecost

### TODAY'S THEME

We are citizens of heaven, gradually making our way home. Before anything was created, and after the end of time, our God continues to reign. All who love him have been promised a share in his Kingdom of heaven.

In both years the flowers need to express the glory of heaven, with a sense of majesty, light and joy. Go for a large scale, either arranged like a sheaf of abundance, or like a brilliant star.

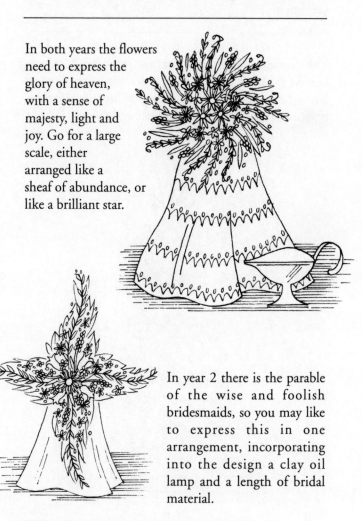

In year 2 there is the parable of the wise and foolish bridesmaids, so you may like to express this in one arrangement, incorporating into the design a clay oil lamp and a length of bridal material.

# Notes

# Notes

# Notes

# Notes

# Notes